# WOULD YOU RATHER...?

*The Romantic Conversation Game for Couples*

## LOVE AND ROMANCE EDITION

J.R. James

Spice up your love life even more, and explore all the discussion books for couples by J.R. James:

## Love and Relationship Books for Couples

*Would You Rather...? The Romantic Conversation Game for Couples (Love and Romance Edition)*

## Sexy Game Books for Couples

*Would You Rather...? The Naughty Conversation Game for Couples (Hot and Sexy Edition)*

*Truth or Dare? The Sexy Game of Naughty Choices (Hot and Wild Edition)*

*Never Have I Ever... An Exciting and Sexy Game for Adults (Hot and Dirty Edition)*

## Sexy Discussion Books for Couples

*Let's Talk Sexy: Essential Conversation Starters to Explore Your Lover's Secret Desires and Transform Your Sex Life*

All **THREE** *Let's Talk About...* sexy question books in one massive volume for one low price. Save now!

*Let's Talk About... Sexual Fantasies and Desires: Questions and Conversation Starters for Couples Exploring Their Sexual Interests*

*Let's Talk About... Non-Monogamy: Questions and Conversation Starters for Couples Exploring Open Relationships, Swinging, or Polyamory*

*Let's Talk About... Kinks and Fetishes: Questions and Conversation Starters for Couples Exploring Their Sexual Wild Side*

# Sign up for our mailing list and be entered to win a FREE copy of any of the sexy question books by J.R. James. New winner selected every month!

## Sign up here:
https://mailchi.mp/a75ed05fd334/jrjames

# HOW TO PLAY THE GAME

The rules for this game are very simple:

There needs to be at least two people to play, so get your spouse, partner, or significant other and create a space that's conducive to conversation. (This is an ideal game for a date night at home or while on vacation, as those provide the perfect opportunities to focus on each other.)

Each page has a hypothetical question that begins with "Would you rather...?" and ends with two choices. Take turns asking and answering the questions. **You must choose one of the options, and no skipping the questions.**

As you spend time discussing the answers, you'll soon you'll find yourselves smiling, laughing, and enjoying intimate conversation with each other. Who knows? You may even discover new possibilities for your relationship. Have fun! Everyone wins as long as you play the game together!

*Enjoy!*

# <u>1</u>
## *Would you rather…*

Have a quiet, candlelit dinner with your partner,

OR

Participate in a heart pounding, adrenalin-filled date together, such as sky-diving?

# 2
## *Would you rather...*

Have your lover massage
your feet with oil,

## OR

Or enjoy a long, hot bath
with them instead?

# 3
## *Would you rather...*

Try something new and exciting in the bedroom,

OR

Take up a new hobby together with your partner?

## <u>4</u>
## *Would you rather...*

Receive an unexpected gift from your significant other,

OR

Spend the evening sipping wine and talking together?

# 5

*Would you rather…*

Go on more "romantic" dates,

OR

Go on more "fun" dates?

# <u>6</u>

## *Would you rather…*

Kiss more often,

OR

Hug more often?

# 7

## *Would you rather…*

Receive a thoughtful, sweet phone call from your partner,

OR

Be surprised by a flirty, sexy text from them?

# 8

## *Would you rather...*

Visit somewhere new with your lover on a weekend getaway,

### OR

Have an intimate, quiet weekend at home with just the two of you?

# 9

*Would you rather…*

Be kissed over every
square inch of your body,

OR

Hear naughty things
whispered in your ear?

# *10*

## *Would you rather…*

Enjoy more laughs with
your partner,

## OR

Have more "serious"
discussions with them?

# 11

## *Would you rather...*

Have more foreplay in the bedroom,

OR

Cuddle everywhere else more often?

# _12_

## _Would you rather..._

Watch a movie while snuggling on the sofa,

## OR

Go out on the town for an evening of drinks and dancing?

# 13

*Would you rather…*

Have your significant other help you with tasks that need to get done,

OR

Hear them tell you how much they love you every day?

## <u>14</u>

# *Would you rather...*

Talk about sexual desires more often,

OR

Talk about plans and goals more often?

# <u>15</u>

*Would you rather...*

Have your partner cook
your favorite dinner,

OR

Surprise you by cleaning
your car?

# _**16**_
## _Would you rather…_

Have more variety in the bedroom,

OR

Have more date nights?

# <u>17</u>
## *Would you rather...*

Have your lover listen to you talk about your day,

OR

Have them give you a back massage?

# _18_

## _Would you rather…_

Watch a movie that you and your significant other both enjoy,

### OR

Watch a theatrical production that neither of you have seen before?

# **_19_**

## *Would you rather...*

Get hugs from the front,

OR

Get hugs from behind?

# **20**

*Would you rather…*

Use chocolate syrup during sex,


OR


Use whipped cream?

# <u>21</u>
## *Would you rather…*

Have sex that is slow, gentle, and can last for hours,

OR

Have sex that's passionate and energetic, but doesn't last as long?

# <u>22</u>

## *Would you rather...*

Hear a compliment from your lover,

OR

Get a hug and a kiss?

# 23

## *Would you rather…*

Hold hands with your partner,

### OR

Wrap your arms around each other?

# *24*

# *Would you rather…*

Be teased with suggestive words,

OR

Be teased with suggestive actions?

# $\underline{25}$
## *Would you rather…*

Wake up to breakfast in bed,

OR

Wake up to gentle kisses?

# **26**
*Would you rather…*

Cuddle while falling
asleep,

OR

Cuddle when first waking
up?

# <u>27</u>

## *Would you rather…*

Hear "I love you" every day,

OR

*See* through actions how much your partner loves you throughout the day?

# **_28_**

## _Would you rather…_

Make your lover moan,

OR

Make them laugh?

# **29**
## *Would you rather...*

Go on a surprise road trip with your significant other,

OR

Plan out a vacation together?

# _30_

## _Would you rather…_

Come home to lit candles and dinner on the table,

OR

Come home to rose petals strewn everywhere and champagne waiting for you?

# <u>*31*</u>
## *Would you rather...*

Cuddle on a blanket at the beach in summer,

OR

Cuddle in front of a roaring fireplace in the middle of winter?

# <u>32</u>
## *Would you rather…*

Take a shower with your lover,

OR

Take a bath with them?

# **33**

*Would you rather…*

Hear your partner tell you about their fantasies,

OR

Tell them about all of *your* fantasies?

# *34*

## *Would you rather...*

Have more sex in the daytime,

OR

Have more sex in the night?

# 35
## *Would you rather…*

Read a love poem from
your significant other,

OR

Receive a thoughtful gift
from them?

# <u>36</u>
## *Would you rather…*

Ride bikes together,

OR

Go on long walks?

# _37_

## _Would you rather…_

Cook dinner together as a couple,

OR

Make breakfast together?

# *38*

## *Would you rather…*

Have your partner comfort you when you're feeling sad,

### OR

Have them try and cheer you up instead?

## <u>39</u>
*Would you rather…*

Have your toes kissed and teased by your lover,

OR

Have your fingers kissed and teased with their tongue?

# _40_

## _Would you rather..._

Receive an incredibly romantic gesture from your partner,

OR

Try something new and adventurous in bed?

# 41
## *Would you rather...*

Spend less time watching television together,

OR

Spend less time apart?

# 42

## *Would you rather…*

Be sexually intimate in lots of bright lighting,

OR

In complete darkness?

## _43_

_Would you rather…_

Spend a romantic evening in a hotel,

OR

At a Bed and Breakfast?

# 44
## *Would you rather…*

Have a deep conversation
with your partner,

## OR

Have them touch you
passionately?

# 45
## *Would you rather...*

Receive a gift on special occasions,

OR

Have them listen to your problems whenever you need them to?

# <u>46</u>

## *Would you rather...*

Hear your partner say "I truly appreciate you,"

OR

Have them spend a lot of time with you?

# 47

## *Would you rather…*

Have your significant other do a special act of kindness for you,

### OR

Give you a lot of attention throughout the day?

# ___48___

## *Would you rather…*

Do something fun together every day,

OR

Have your partner say sweet things to you every day?

## 49

# *Would you rather…*

Have more intimacy in
your relationship,

OR

Have more meaningful
conversations?

# **50**
## *Would you rather…*

Get a sincere compliment from your lover,

OR

Find out they generously took care of a chore that you don't like doing yourself?

## <u>51</u>

*Would you rather…*

Sit together closely on the sofa every evening,

### OR

Hear your partner tell you how great you look every evening?

# 52
## *Would you rather...*

Receive a generous, expensive gift from your significant other,

### OR

Receive an inexpensive gift that they spent a lot of their time to create?

# 53

*Would you rather...*

Go out on the town for
more dates,

OR

Have more at home dates?

# <u>54</u>
## *Would you rather…*

Your partner serenade you
with a romantic song,

OR

Write you a heartfelt letter?

# 55

*Would you rather…*

Go to a sporting event with your significant other,

OR

Go to a concert together?

# 56

## *Would you rather…*

Receive a romantic gift on your anniversary,

## OR

Receive a romantic gift on your birthday?

# 57

*Would you rather…*

Take a weeklong vacation with your partner,

OR

Have them happily help you with your daily chores for a month?

# 58

## *Would you rather…*

Overhear your partner saying something sweet about you to their friends,

### OR

Catch them secretly making a thoughtful gift for you?

# <u>59</u>

*Would you rather…*

Have me be more dominant in the bedroom,

OR

Have me be more submissive when we're intimate?

# **60**

*Would you rather…*

Watch a movie about our personal love story,

OR

Read a book about it?

# <u>61</u>

*Would you rather…*

Stay up all night talking to your partner,

OR

Stay out all night dancing?

# **<u>62</u>**

## *Would you rather...*

Relive one of our favorite moments together,

OR

Relive the first time we kissed?

# **<u>63</u>**

## *Would you rather…*

Have more foreplay in
your life,

OR

Have more sexual
intimacy?

# <u>64</u>

## *Would you rather…*

Give up kissing for the rest of your life,

OR

Give up any foreplay?

# **<u>65</u>**

## *Would you rather…*

Make out under the stars while camping,

OR

Hold each other while watching a sunset on the beach?

# <u>66</u>

## *Would you rather...*

Give forehead kisses,

OR

Get forehead kisses?

# **67**

## *Would you rather...*

Stay up late together,

OR

Get up early together?

# **68**

*Would you rather…*

Receive a sweet text from your partner while they're at work,

OR

Send your partner a thoughtful text message while you're at work?

## **<u>69</u>**

# *Would you rather…*

Fool around in a hot tub,

OR

Make out in a darkened
movie theater?

# <u>70</u>

## *Would you rather…*

Enjoy more long walks together,

OR

Take more long drives together?

## 71

### *Would you rather…*

Take a vacation somewhere really sunny and warm,

OR

Somewhere cold, but romantic?

# 72

*Would you rather...*

Receive a surprise back massage from your partner,

OR

An unexpected foot massage?

# _73_

_Would you rather…_

Be teased with ice cubes during foreplay,

OR

Teased with lots of soft kisses on your neck?

# <u>74</u>

*Would you rather…*

Have a long sexy phone conversation with your partner,

OR

Have them send you flirty texts throughout the day?

# 75

## *Would you rather…*

Have your significant other throw you a surprise birthday party,

OR

Have them plan an intimate birthday weekend for just the two of you?

# <u>76</u>
## *Would you rather…*

Go on a picnic together early in the morning as the sun rises,

OR

Late in the evening as the sun sets?

# 77

## *Would you rather…*

Give your lover a sexy dance,

OR

Give them a sexy body massage?

# 78

## *Would you rather…*

Your partner be the one who laughs a lot,

### OR

Be the one who always makes *you* laugh?

# <u>79</u>

## *Would you rather…*

Wear matching outfits for a week,

OR

Wear matching shoes?

# _**80**_
## _Would you rather…_

Watch a terribly made
movie together,


OR


Watch a comedy?

## _81_

_Would you rather..._

Only be able to kiss with your eyes open,

OR

Only be able to have sex with your eyes closed?

# *82*

## *Would you rather…*

Be kissed and teased while blindfolded,

OR

Or while gently tied up?

# *83*

## *Would you rather…*

Give up cuddling for a month,

OR

Go without kissing for a month?

## _84_

## _Would you rather…_

Be teased with your lover's lips,

OR

Be teased with their tongue?

# <u>*85*</u>

*Would you rather…*

Take more photos of each other,

## OR

Record more videos of you two together?

# 86

## *Would you rather…*

Throw a New Year's Eve party with your significant other,

OR

Spend the holiday evening alone with them?

# 87

## *Would you rather...*

Get an unexpected hug and kiss from your lover,

### OR

Get an unexpected gift from them?

# <u>**88**</u>
## *Would you rather...*

Make out with your partner in an unusual setting,

OR

Make love to them somewhere familiar?

# 89

*Would you rather…*

Refer to your partner only
by their "pet name" for one
month,

## OR

Have them only call you by
your pet name for three
months?

# <u>90</u>

## *Would you rather…*

Roleplay with your lover,

OR

Use a new toy in the bedroom?

# 91
*Would you rather…*

Listen to more live music
with your partner,

OR

Eat at more fancy
restaurants together?

# **_92_**

## _Would you rather..._

Take a sexy class with your significant other,

## OR

Learn how to ballroom dance with them?

# **_93_**

## _Would you rather…_

Star in a television show together,

OR

Perform in a live play or musical together?

## <u>94</u>

*Would you rather...*

Not be able to see during sex,


OR


Not be able to hear?

# <u>95</u>

*Would you rather…*

Disagree with your partner more often, but have frequent, passionate love-making,

## OR

Agree with each other more frequently, but have increased boredom in the bedroom?

# **96**

*Would you rather…*

Get a tattoo of your partner's face somewhere on your body,

OR

Have them get a tattoo of you?

## 97

*Would you rather…*

Your partner find you even more attractive than they already do,

OR

Have them find you even more intelligent?

# <u>98</u>

## *Would you rather...*

Fulfill a partner's sexual fantasy,

OR

Ask them to fulfill one of your fantasies?

# **99**

*Would you rather…*

Spend more quiet time together,

OR

Spend more time doing activities together?

# _<u>100</u>_

## _Would you rather..._

Take a day off in the middle of the week with your partner, just so the two of you can hang out for the day,

## OR

Give up all electronic devices for a weekend, so the two of you can focus on each other?

# <u>*101*</u>
## *Would you rather…*

Have more long love-making sessions,

OR

Have more "quickies?"

# 102
*Would you rather…*

Be more compassionate and understanding in your relationship,

OR

Be more thoughtful and kind?

# *103*

## *Would you rather…*

Read a book together,

OR

Play a board or card game together?

# <u>*104*</u>

## *Would you rather...*

Increase the amount of texts we send each other,

### OR

Talk on the phone more often?

# <u>105</u>
## *Would you rather…*

Laugh uncontrollably
during foreplay,

OR

Laugh during sex?

# <u>*106*</u>
## *Would you rather…*

Take a trip around the world in a cruise ship,

### OR

Take a trip around the world by plane (and foot)?

# _107_

_Would you rather…_

Have more sex in the morning,

OR

Have more sex in the afternoon?

# ***108***

*Would you rather…*

Make out more,

OR

Snuggle in bed more?

# _109_

## _Would you rather…_

Play a new sport together,

OR

Cook a meal together?

# _**110**_

## _Would you rather..._

Sleep in the nude together,

OR

Sleep in sexy pajamas?

Spice up your love life even more, and explore all the discussion books for couples by J.R. James:

## Love and Relationship Books for Couples

*Would You Rather...? The Romantic Conversation Game for Couples (Love and Romance Edition)*

## Sexy Game Books for Couples

*Would You Rather...? The Naughty Conversation Game for Couples (Hot and Sexy Edition)*

*Truth or Dare? The Sexy Game of Naughty Choices (Hot and Wild Edition)*

*Never Have I Ever... An Exciting and Sexy Game for Adults (Hot and Dirty Edition)*

## Sexy Discussion Books for Couples

*Let's Talk Sexy: Essential Conversation Starters to Explore Your Lover's Secret Desires and Transform Your Sex Life*

All **THREE** *Let's Talk About...* sexy question books in one massive volume for one low price. Save now!

*Let's Talk About... Sexual Fantasies and Desires: Questions and Conversation Starters for Couples Exploring Their Sexual Interests*

*Let's Talk About... Non-Monogamy: Questions and Conversation Starters for Couples Exploring Open Relationships, Swinging, or Polyamory*

*Let's Talk About... Kinks and Fetishes: Questions and Conversation Starters for Couples Exploring Their Sexual Wild Side*

# Sign up for our mailing list and be entered to win a FREE copy of any of the sexy question books by J.R. James. New winner selected every month!

## Sign up here:
https://mailchi.mp/a75ed05fd334/jrjames

# ABOUT THE AUTHOR

J.R. James is a health professional who has a passion for bringing couples closer together and recharging their sexual intimacy. Erotic discussion is a powerfully sexy thing, and his conversation starter books have helped many couples reach new and sexually exciting heights in their relationships!

Sexy conversation with your partner is a magical, bonding experience. Through these best-selling question books, couples can find an easy way to engage in open and honest sexual discussion with each other. The result is a relationship that is both erotically charged and sexually liberating.

Printed in Great Britain
by Amazon